Yo-Yo Tricks

The 100 Coolest Tricks For Your Yo-Yo

Copyright 2018 by : Ibrahim Martinez All rights reserved.

This document is geared towards providing exact and reliable information in regards to the topic and issue covered. The publication is sold on the idea that the publisher is not required to render an accounting, officially permitted, or otherwise, qualified services. If advice is necessary, legal or professional, a practiced individual in the profession should be ordered.

- From a Declaration of Principles which was accepted and approved equally by a Committee of the American Bar Association and a Committee of Publishers and Associations.

In no way is it legal to reproduce, duplicate, or transmit any part of this document by either electronic means or in printed format. Recording of this publication is strictly prohibited and any storage of this document is not allowed unless with written permission from the publisher. All rights reserved.

The information provided herein is stated to be truthful and consistent, in that any liability, in terms of inattention or otherwise, by any usage or abuse of any policies, processes, or directions contained within is the solitary and utter responsibility of the recipient reader. Under no circumstances will any legal responsibility or blame be held against the publisher for any reparation, damages, or monetary loss due to the information herein, either directly or indirectly. Respective authors own all copyrights not held by the publisher.

Introduction

If you've seen a cool yo-yo trick, you might immediately want to know how it's done. There are so many cool yo-yo tricks that you will be able to impress people for years with them!

One of the great things about yo-yo tricks is that they are still interesting and exciting even after they have been explained. Many people are disappointed when they learn about the secrets of their favorite magicians for the first time. Conjurers, after all, are using misdirection in order to fool you. This is not the case with a yo-yo trick.

A yo-yo trick might seem almost mystical in its fluidity. However, this is still something that is largely a matter of skill. You need to become dexterous enough to pull off a lot of these moves.

Yo-yo tricks have the advantage of building on themselves. If you know certain moves, you will be able to figure out a lot of others. It's important to learn some of the fundamental yo-yo moves first, and from there, you can proceed to learn the sort of moves that could make you a yo-yo star!

Explaining a yo-yo trick is often complicated. It can be difficult to visualize what's happening. However, if you are a person who is used to using a yo-yo in the first place, you will probably find that the instructions will be a little bit more intuitive for you in general.

Factors That Influence the Success of Yo-Yo Tricks

Many people might have a hard time performing certain yo-yo tricks. They might be under the impression that this is purely due to their own level of skill and not the yo-yo that they use. However, some yo-yo toys are actually better for certain tricks than others.

If you want to perform a range of different yo-yo tricks, you are better off having both a thicker yo-yo and a narrower yo-yo on hand. If you can get yo-yo toys that exist in a wide range of sizes, that will actually be that much better.

Wider yo-yo toys are much better for flips and tricks that involve flips of any kind. Narrower yo-yo toys are often better when it comes to tricks that involve loops of some kind. If you don't have much hand strength, however, you might always find that a trick that involves a narrower and therefore lighter yo-yo might be better.

If you have more hand strength, you are going to have an advantage when it comes to each and every yo-yo trick. Having flexible wrists can be just as important. However, the yo-yo can feel surprisingly heavy during the yo-yo trick. People need to be able to exercise enough control during the actual yo-yo trick, and hand strength and flexibility will help. Still, a wide range of people are still able to learn yo-yo tricks in general, so no one should feel that the skill is just out of reach forever.

People who are left-handed or right-handed will also have different advantages when it comes to using yo-yo toys. People who do certain yo-yo tricks will find that the yo-yo string will continue to get tighter and tighter if they are right-handed. On the other hand, people who are left-handed will often find that the string will keep on getting looser and looser as they perform certain tricks. Technically, this will put both groups at a disadvantage in some cases.

Finding a way to be ambidextrous with a yo-yo will help almost anyone get better with it. People will indeed need to use both of their hands in order to perform certain yo-yo tricks. You can't just get away with using your dominant hand in some cases. Finding a way to use both of your hands at the right time can make all the difference in the world in most cases. It will open you up to a lot of different new tricks right away.

If you can make both hands your potential yo-yo hand, that will work out much better for you. Generally speaking, people will use their dominant hands as their yo-yo hands. They might use their other hands as their free hands. Depending on the yo-yo trick, however, the free hand might do more work and it might be the hand that has to perform with more dexterity.

People who are naturally good at using both of their hands in complicated ways are automatically going to have more of an advantage when it comes to all yo-yo tricks. If there is any meta skill that you should try to learn in order to excel at yo-yo tricks, it is ambidexterity.

You should also try to train your wrists when it comes to flexibility. This will make it easier for you to be able to really take advantage of the range of motion that your wrists can achieve. If you can do this, the number of yo-yo tricks that you can learn will expand right away.

Fundamental Yo-Yo Tricks

1. Gravity Pull

It just doesn't get any more fundamental than the Gravity Pull. This is a trick that is so basic that some people watching might not even think of it as a trick in the first place. However, it is a very real trick. If you've ever thrown a yo-yo before, you will probably notice that it is a harder move than you might think just from looking at it.

The yo-yo is tossed downward in a Gravity Pull, and then people cause the yo-yo to wind up again right into their hands. When this trick is done in a swift enough manner, it can tend to look really impressive to a lot of people.

If the slipknot is not tightly wound around your middle finger, it can be a problem. The yo-yo has to be initially positioned in the center of a person's hand. From there, people will be able to complete the gravity pull. Once you can do this, you're on your way to much more advanced yo-yo tricks!

2. The Forward Pass

With this yo-yo trick, you will automatically read as more experienced than a lot of other yo-yo users. You will throw the yo-yo outward, at an angle away from the body. Your hand will be facing downward during this part of the process, with the palm of your hand facing the ground.

During the throw, you turn your hand over so the palm is facing upwards. That way, the yo-yo will land in your hand in a very slick manner. Subtly changing the position of your hand without affecting the movement of the yo-yo will take a little bit of skill. Once you do that, it should be that much easier for you to complete this yo-yo trick and many of the others.

3. Sleeper

This is a trick that you need to learn if you're going to do many other yo-yo tricks. If you don't know the Sleeper, you will be hugely limited in terms of the yo-yo tricks that you can perform. This is a trick that is easier than it looks. You just need to incorporate enough control, and you'll be there.

In the Sleeper, the yo-yo is thrown down and the string has been extended all the way. Normally, this is the point where the yo-yo will bounce up again. However, in this case, the yo-yo will stay in one place at the end of the string and spin around.

You're going to need to use a lot of energy in order to make this work, and the string has to be in the right position. The string on the yo-yo needs to be aligned over the top of the yo-yo when the palm is up, and this will create a situation where the yo-yo will roll off the hands in the right way.

Once you learn how to throw the Sleeper in the best possible way with the right amount of energy, you will be able to perform a wide range of different yo-yo tricks.

4. Around the World

Once you have learned the Forward Pass, you will be able to move onto the Around the World trick. This is also a trick that requires a firm knowledge of the Sleeper. You basically throw a Forward Pass, and then cause the yo-yo to make a complete rotation back to your hand.

The yo-yo will make that rotation back to your hand in the Sleeper mode the whole time, so you need to be skilled at making the yo-yo sleep in order to make this trick possible. There is a risk of the yo-yo string getting tangled during the Around the World motion, and you need to learn the dexterity to stop that from happening. Once you do, this is one of the most exciting yo-yo tricks that you can try, and it makes you look really skilled with the toy!

5. Walk the Dog

People have probably seen this yo-yo trick before. People need to be skilled at the sleeper trick in order to do this one. It requires a solid sleeper in order to work. You start off by putting a strong sleeper into motion. You then allow the sleeper to make contact with the ground in a way that is delicate, so you don't end up disrupting the trick or the movement of the yo-yo.

The sleeper needs a really energetic toss in order for this trick to work, or there won't be enough energy to make the yo-yo 'walk.' The yo-yo will not be able to perform the walking motion on the ground if it is not spinning fast enough. Friction from the ground will disrupt the amount of energy that the yo-yo will have for the sake of spinning. That is energy that you need to provide for it.

As the yo-yo moves away from you on the ground, its spinning will really make it seem like it is walking away from you, which can be interesting to see. This is a trick that will make you think of a dog walking, at least when it is performed correctly.

You might want to 'walk' the yo-yo in front of you, which is a common way of doing this trick. You could also have the yo-yo walk on the side of you. Some people might walk the yo-yo between their legs as well, which requires even more control and which can look more impressive. One way or another, the Walk the Dog trick is a favorite for a lot of people.

6. Breakaway

This is a trick that is almost identical to the Around the World trick. In fact, some people might say that it's easier. The only real difference is the direction involved. You throw a Forward Pass with this trick and have the yo-yo sleep. However, with the Around the World trick, you throw a complete three hundred and sixty degree circle all the way around. With the Breakaway, you throw a semi-circle in front of yourself.

7. Pinwheel

You will need to know how to perform the Breakaway yo-yo trick in order to then perform the Pinwheel yo-yo trick. After all, you do start by throwing the Breakaway as your first move. This is a yo-yo trick that you will be able to perform in front of your body or on the right or left side of your body, making it a somewhat versatile stage trick.

Essentially, what you do is throw the Breakaway and grab the string at about the halfway point with your other hand, at which point the yo-yo will just dangle if you don't do anything else. You might want to practice the trick that way in the beginning, in fact. Then, have the other half of the string, the half that has the yo-yo, start spinning around in a big circle in order to complete this yo-yo trick. In order to create this sort of spinning motion, you are going to need to rotate your other hand around in a circle. This might remind you of a cowboy swinging a lasso.

This is a yo-yo trick that should be fairly easy for the people who are used to doing the Breakaway yo-yo trick overall. This is a trick that is all about timing and making sure that you catch the right part of the yo-yo string at the right time. You also need to make sure that the rotating part of the string is not going to form a circle that is too big. Otherwise, might might actually end up hitting yourself in the face. The swinging motion is also more dramatic if the rotation circle looks somewhat smaller. Catching the string at the halfway point should be enough to make this happen.

8. Rock the Baby

Most people look at this trick and they assume that it's very difficult. For the most part, it mainly involves throwing a Sleeper. The tough part is actually creating the triangle where you 'rock the baby.' You basically throw a Sleeper in a conventional manner. After that, you grab the string in such a way that it forms a triangle around the yo-yo while the yo-yo rocks back and forth.

It's a good idea to practice this trick using an inert yo-yo at first. You need to find a way to form the triangle in the right way and at the right time. It basically involves grabbing the string at the halfway point down the string, and then grabbing the next halfway point, and forming the triangle that way.

As you might guess, this is very much the sort of move that can go awry. You could end up getting the yo-yo string tangled up, and this is always tricky to fix. Once you get the hang of this trick by using an inert yo-yo, you should be able to Rock the Baby using a yo-yo that is in a Sleeper mode.

Intermediate Yo-Yo Tricks

People will disagree about whether or not these tricks truly count as intermediate. Some people will consider them basic enough tricks that beginners will be able to use them. However, these are still tricks that are tough for a lot of people, and they tend to look impressive to a lot of onlookers as well.

Some of these tricks will give you the opportunity to learn the skills that you need in order to take on some of the more complex yo-yo tricks. These are the tricks that will be hard to even follow as you are watching them. The intermediate yo-yo tricks are much easier to learn intuitively, and that will help a lot of people when it comes to the basic and immediate learning process.

9. Around the Corner

This is a string trick, actually, making it a yo-yo trick that should fall within another specific category. You essentially just throw the yo-yo in the usual way, but you have the top of your elbow break the yo-yo string so the yo-yo string is balancing on the top of your elbow briefly. This should cause the yo-yo to pull forward towards your body.

You then grab the yo-yo string at the point where it is close to your body using your free hand. This is the motion that should cause the yo-yo to swing back in the opposite direction. As a result, you should be able to catch it when it makes its trip back around your arm.

Pulling the yo-yo when the yo-yo is on its first revolution should be able to give the yo-yo the energy that it needs in order to make it on its journey all the way back around your arm. You need to be able to create this energy, or you will not be able to get the yo-yo all the way around your arm. This is another trick that is all about timing, and with the right dexterity, it is a crowd pleasing trick.

10. Lindy Loop

This is a yo-yo trick that is very similar to the Pinwheel trick. However, in this case, you do not just swing the yo-yo in a complete rotation. You start to do so in the manner of the Pinwheel trick, which can be a lot of fun. However, it's like you start to do the Pinwheel trick, and then you stop it. You repeat this process. Then, you throw the yo-yo up in the air, and you catch it again.

When you catch the yo-yo with your free hand, you more or less stop it with just a single extended finger. You also stop the yo-yo and then roll the yo-yo back around again for the second stop, so the string is going to wrap around your finger to a greater extent. You then can just quickly rotate your finger around in the opposite direction in order to unravel everything and cause the move to undo itself in an exciting manner. Once that is finished, you can throw the yo-yo up in the air and roll it back.

You need to be good enough at doing the Pinwheel trick in order to make that work. However, as Intermediate tricks go, this one is relatively easy to accomplish.

11. Brain Twister

The name of this yo-yo trick is going to make it sound really complex. It's actually a trick that people can accomplish in only a few moves, so it is not as complex as people might think.

You start by throwing the yo-yo in the usual way. Then, using your free hand, you pull the yo-yo up at an angle so it's dangling slightly. You then lower the yo-yo, threading it back through the string like you're about to almost sloppily roll it up in the string again.

You need to thread it very loosely in order for this part to work. From there, you flip the yo-yo over in the complete opposite direction. Then, you open the span of your arms further in order to flip the yo-yo outwardly in the opposite direction in order to make it loose and to more or less undo the entire trick.

Part of the appeal of this trick lies in the fact that it is difficult to even follow what the yo-yo is doing when the yo-yo trick is fully in motion. You have to watch carefully in order to see what the skilled yo-yo user is trying to do with the toy. Once you explain the yo-yo trick, it seems fairly straightforward, of course. However, as you get to that point, it's easier for you to confuse other people as they're watching you perform the yo-yo trick!

12. Eiffel Tower

This is another yo-yo trick that is primarily a string trick. It's much simpler than it appears to be at first glance. Like a lot of Intermediate yo-yo tricks, it's more impressive than it might initially appear, which is part of the appeal.

You put the yo-yo into a Sleeper mode throughout the duration of this trick. Once you throw the yo-yo, you grab it by the string just where it is close to the hand that you are using to throw the yo-yo. Using your free hand, you then pull the yo-yo string upward towards yourself so that it creates something of a loop.

You then lower that loop down and twist it to the side as you lower it, so it creates something of an hourglass shape. You then pull that new hourglass shape downwards in order to grab some of the remainder of the yo-yo string. You then pull it upward towards you again at an angle.

Using the hand that has the yo-yo, you then twist the string to the side. This should give you the chance to get a shape that looks somewhat like the Eiffel Tower as you hold it up for everyone to see. It also looks kind of like a star that has its 'arms' cut off, so only the bottom and middle points are visible. There should be a little triangle in the center of the Eiffel Tower shape that should allow you to get the right geometrical configuration and that will make this shape more polished than it might appear to be at first glance.

13. The Elevator

With this yo-yo trick, you just need to throw down the yo-yo in the normal manner. You then grab the yo-yo by the string about halfway down the string and hold the yo-yo so the string is in the center. You then roll the yo-yo upwards along the string so it gets higher and higher until it actually reaches your free hand as you spread your hands apart more and more.

You might actually hear the yo-yo winding at certain points during the actual yo-yo trick, which is just the sort of thing that can make the name of the yo-yo trick seem more appropriate. This is a yo-yo trick that requires you to catch the yo-yo in the right place at the right time, and you have to make sure that you're winding it tightly enough in order for it all to work. However, this is the sort of thing that you should be able to accomplish with the right dexterity.

14. Time Warp

You need to be skilled at the Around the World trick in order to become skilled at this one. This is basically a double yo-yo trick. It's a matter of doing the Around the World motion and then doing that same Around the World yo-yo trick, only backwards. In order to make this trick work, when the yo-yo comes back to you, you need to sort of let the yo-yo bounce off of your hand.

The trick is to make it look like the Time Warp is all a part of a single motion. If you break it up, it won't look as impressive. When you're still trying to learn this trick, it might be acceptable to break it up into two motions. However, the Time Warp is still more impressive if you allow it all to become part of a single flowing motion and the yo-yo just bounces off of your hand.

15. Flip

This is actually not just a yo-yo trick. It is actually a fundamental yo-yo move that is going to help you with a lot of other yo-yo tricks. However, it is a lot harder than some of the yo-yo tricks that can form the basis of other yo-yo tricks, so it is still worth regarding it as an Intermediate yo-yo move.

With this trick or with tricks that involve flips, it is ideal to use a wide yo-yo. Still, people who are experienced with yo-yo toys typically want to be able to perform all tricks with all of their yo-yo toys, and so it makes sense for people to not really take the size of the yo-yo into account all that much when learning. However, you might want to practice flips with a wider yo-yo at first in order to get the hang of it all.

Flips more or less involve retracting and extending the yo-yo in the normal way. However, you change the position of your hand as you do it so the yo-yo appears to just sort of bounce off your hand, traveling in a different direction.

This is one of the many different yo-yo tricks that will more or less involve a single hand. You might use your free hand for balance, but all of the real action is happening as a result of your 'yo-yo' hand here. This is one of the many yo-yo tricks that is about dexterity more than anything else, since there are not a lot of steps to memorize.

16. Snap Wind

This is a fun yo-yo trick that will allow you to create some really interesting visual effects. With the Snap Wind yo-yo trick, you hold the yo-yo in your hand. Then, you throw it up in the air directly above you in something of a clear and straight vertical motion.

At that point, the string of the yo-yo will look as if it has waves, and the yo-yo will start to wind itself back up again. However, since you have the yo-yo going in a different direction then you usually would, the yo-yo is going to wind itself up in a way that is more interesting and that will appear more dramatic in most cases.

You have to sort of flip the yo-yo upward in order to create this motion. It does indeed need to snap, and you need to give it the energy that it takes to cause the yo-yo to snap upward. However, this part of the process should be easier than it looks. This is another trick that is largely about dexterity, and not necessarily just understanding all of the necessary steps and components.

17. Forward Toss

While this is a component of a lot of different and more advanced yo-yo tricks, it is also accurate to say that it is something of a trick in its own right. This is basically a trick that involves you throwing the yo-yo out at an angle and having it sort of bounce back to you in a very fluid motion. You can use a narrower and lighter yo-yo for this trick, and that is often going to be better than some of the other yo-yo toys that you might use for it. Still, it's a good idea to just practice the Forward Toss in general.

18. Loop

A lot of different yo-yo tricks will involve looping in their own right. With this trick, you basically cause the yo-yo to spin around at an angle by using your yo-yo hand to create the right motions. It will look like the yo-yo is moving around in a circle at a diagonal angle away from you. This is a yo-yo trick where a narrower or lighter yo-yo is often better than a wider one. You will also be able to learn a lot of great advanced tricks if you can master this one.

19. Winding the String

This is certainly one of the most useful yo-yo tricks that you can learn, and it more or less involves winding up the string in a way that is a lot faster and more impressive. This is a method of winding up the yo-yo that looks like the yo-yo is practically spinning upwards into your hand. In order to do this, you basically do need to get the yo-yo to spin upwards into your hand. Since a lot of people will wind up the yo-yo manually, this is still a useful action that will read as a yo-yo trick to a lot of people with less experience. This is also certainly a move that will work as a component of a lot of different yo-yo tricks at the end of the day.

20. Finger Grind

You can learn a lot of great yo-yo tricks if you can master the Finger Grind. A yo-yo trick grind involves the physical yo-yo itself touching a particular part of your body. With the Finger Grind in particular, you throw the yo-yo in the normal way but you toss it upwards so that the yo-yo makes contact with your finger. This yo-yo should then spin on its own axis on your finger so that it looks like you have this mechanical spinning device on your finger that is still going.

Finding a way to pull this off can be really helpful if you want to learn a lot of advanced yo-yo tricks. It also looks like a fairly impressive yo-yo trick in its own right, which makes it all the more useful for the people who are trying to find a way to quickly 'wow' their audience. The fact that it is possible to do this in almost a single motion makes it all better.

21. Palm Grind

This is a yo-yo trick that is very similar to a Finger Grind. However, in this case, the yo-yo is spinning around on its axis back and forth in the palm of your hand. With this one, you have to throw the yo-yo in the first place in order to make it work. You basically catch it in the palm of your hand in order to make this particular grind work.

This can be easier than a Finger Grind, because you are catching the yo-yo in an area that has more space. People are also more used to catching things in the palm of their hands as a matter of course. However, you still have to catch it in such a way that the act of catching it will not disrupt the spinning that can occur.

22. Off-Axis Finger Grind

While this yo-yo trick, you are once again trying to catch the actual yo-yo on your finger. However, in this case, you try to catch the yo-yo on the tip of your free hand's index finger so that it is more or less rotating around the tip of the index finger. This might remind you of the motion involving a plate spinning around on a wand or a stick. You really need to be able to catch the yo-yo in the exact right way in order to make a motion like this work, which is definitely no easy task. However, that will make it all the more exceptional when you do manage to pull it off for yourself.

23. Elbow Grind

This is a grind that is very similar to the others. However, with this particular yo-yo trick, the goal is to try to catch the yo-yo on the side of the elbow of your free hand. Some of the more advanced yo-yo tricks will require you to use your whole body, and this is a yo-yo trick that is good preparation for all of that. This is a yo-yo trick that can be somewhat less comfortable to try in a lot of ways, since you do have to catch the yo-yo on a fleshier area than usual.

However, it is still worthwhile to try something like this. You should try to practice this and all of the other grinds using a plastic yo-yo instead of a metal yo-yo for the sake of safety. Some people with more experience might be able to perform something like this with a lot of different yo-yo toys, but you have to work up to that point.

24. Bounce Off

With this yo-yo trick, you start by creating a little loop manually with your free hand as the entire yo-yo string is stretched out in front of you. You then bounce the yo-yo off of that part of the string. You then hook the string with your first finger.

Then, you will swing the yo-yo over, catch the yo-yo in a grind on the outside of your yo-yo hand, and you can then bounce the entire yo-yo back in order to complete the trick. This is a fun and fairly basic yo-yo trick to learn, but it does require you to master your grinds first, which can make it harder than it looks and which elevates it from being something of a basic yo-yo trick.

25. Upward Side Mount

This is a yo-yo trick that will work in order to correct side mount yo-yo tricks that have failed in some way. If it looks like the yo-yo string has gotten caught on your finger in some way, you just gather up the rest of your fingers in order to more or less flip the string upward in order to get the yo-yo back into the right position. This can create a situation where the apparent failure actually appears to be impressive to a lot of people in spite of everything, and it can work as a yo-yo trick in its own right.

26. Bent Side Mount

You can correct side mount yo-yo tricks that have failed in other ways. You more or less creatively bend your hands in order to untangle the side mount that has partly become caught in your hands. If you do this quickly enough, it will appear dexterous. It also does require a degree of dexterity in order to make something like this work in the first place, and that should help most of the people involved who are trying to find a way to make a new yo-yo trick out of an apparent mishap with the yo-yo string.

27. Point Five Mount

You can create an interesting effect with this yo-yo trick, even though it is the sort of trick that is relatively simple. You start by throwing the yo-yo off to the side and then catching it with the index finger of your free hand. You then work the yo-yo string into a triangle and you cause the triangle to gradually flatten as the yo-yo itself falls off to the side. You then let the yo-yo fall back through the yo-yo string and you unravel the yo-yo string and the trick itself in order to complete the whole yo-yo trick. This is a yo-yo trick that has a fairly graceful and interesting effect.

28. Green Triangle

While this is not a yo-yo trick that actually involves anything green, the green classification is useful for the people who are trying to find a way to categorize it. This involves spreading the yo-yo string out and then bouncing it into a strong isosceles triangle configuration. This requires a good amount of finesse, and you ideally will be able to create three distinct sides for the triangle in the first place. If you can do this yo-yo trick quickly enough, you can feel and look like a spider spinning a web and you will feel just as graceful.

29. Mach Five

This is one of the many yo-yo tricks that will require you to quickly come up with a loop. Once you come up with this loop, you will work the yo-yo through it until it looks like the yo-yo is rotating in a circle with a vertical line through it. This will tend to make it look like the yo-yo is traveling very quickly, hence the name. It also might make a person think of an astronaut in zero gravity, which also helps to create the right associations between the move and the name Mach Five.

30. Eli Hop

People will find that this is a yo-yo trick that will look very impressive to a lot of people in spite of the fact that it is a relatively simple trick in a lot of cases. It is a yo-yo hop that involves causing the yo-yo to raise very high in the air at an angle above you and then retracting the yo-yo from there. If you do this in a smooth enough motion, it will be that much easier for you to be able to impress your audience. You need to be good enough at retracting the yo-yo smoothly in order to master the yo-yo trick as well, and that will work.

31. Uppermost Loop

This is a yo-yo trick that appears to be fairly basic in some ways, but it is ultimately a trick that can be more difficult then it looks. It ultimately just involves trying to make the yo-yo loop as highly as you possibly can, while trying to keep it in that position for a comparatively long period of time. You can try to hold that position by throwing the yo-yo upward in the Sleeper mode, although this is very tough as well. Practicing a yo-yo trick like this can help you when it comes to being able to learn some of the most difficult yo-yo tricks in their own right.

Advanced Yo-Yo Tricks

There are plenty of very complex yo-yo tricks that you can try. Some of these tricks are complex in the sense that they require a lot of dexterity, even though the motion itself is not all that hard to follow. Others are advanced yo-yo tricks specifically because it is hard to even see what is happening with the yo-yo during the yo-yo trick itself.

The thing is, both of these types of advanced yo-yo tricks will be very impressive to most of the people watching, especially if they are not all that familiar with yo-yo toys. Some of these tricks require props. Most of them just require a lot of skill and talent with the yo-yo toys in the first place, and you need to get to that point by practicing with the more basic and intermediate tricks a lot.

Most of these advanced yo-yo tricks will only involve a single yo-yo. You might need a second yo-yo for some of them. Wielding two yo-yo toys at once is difficult for the majority of people, but it is something that will almost always make a given yo-yo trick that much more exciting.

32. Casual Trapeze

There are lots of different yo-yo tricks that look vaguely like a person on a trapeze, including this one. You throw the yo-yo, you catch it with your free finger, you cause the yo-yo at the end of the string to rotate as a result. You then cause the yo-yo to bounce back on the string at its center. Then, you fling the other side of the string onto the yo-yo from the opposite direction, looping that part of the string onto the center of the yo-yo. You then swing the loop like the yo-yo is part of the trapeze in order to complete the yo-yo trick.

33. The Spirit's Revenge

This might seem like a dramatic name for a yo-yo trick, but it's still a fun trick. You start by tossing the yo-yo towards the side and then grabbing a loop in the yo-yo string, pulling the string towards you. You then work this into a triangle and you move it to the center of your body. From there, you loop the yo-yo in between the fingers of your other hand before throwing it to the side and then retracting it again. Mastering all of the steps of this yo-yo trick can be difficult, but it is still a visually stunning trick when performed correctly.

34. Plastic Whip

With this yo-yo trick, you make the yo-yo start to sleep at first. Then, you sort of throw it upwards in order to catch part of the yo-yo string in your yo-yo hand in a different way. You try to catch the string so that it looks like you are holding the yo-yo string in something of a v-shape. You then release the yo-yo in order to make it sleep again. Then you throw it upwards again and create a new v-shape using your free hand. You should lift the yo-yo up higher in order to complete that part of the yo-yo trick. If you are able to do this all in a very fluid motion, that should make it even easier for you to create a very good impression with the yo-yo trick.

35. Gyroscopic Flop

This is a fun yo-yo trick that will allow you to really use the yo-yo in a unique way. You start by more or less throwing the yo-yo into a loop. The, you use your hands to tighten the loop in order to make it easier for the yo-yo to move. Then, you try to tighten the loop with your hands enough to make the yo-yo look like it is rotating on its axis just as a result of the tightness of the yo-yo string. This is a yo-yo trick that makes use of the yo-yo itself as the object of attention and curiosity.

36. A Loop With Two Hands

Most of the yo-yo tricks that involve two hands are very difficult for people to perform. It makes sense for people to try to wait until they are ready for the most difficult yo-yo tricks in order to try something like this. This is one of the most basic of all of the two-handed yo-yo tricks, however. It requires two yo-yo toys. You just basically loop with both of them in unison and in creative ways, and this is enough to accomplish the effect. While it seems very simple, it is possible to accomplish a lot with it if you have enough control.

37. Regeneration

You really have to watch a trick like this one closely in order to understand what is actually happening. This is a trick that starts out with a simple throw. Then, you flip the yo-yo. You cause the yo-yo to sleep for a very brief period of time, and then you roll it all back up again.

If you perform the flip part of the yo-yo trick quickly enough, it will almost appear to be invisible. As such, it will look as if the yo-yo has been revived in a way, hence the name. This is a yo-yo trick that will not work for the people who are unused to yo-yo flips. The yo-yo trick tends to work particularly well when the flip is smooth enough. When you can get to that point, the yo-yo trick will work beautifully.

It should be noted that flips are also generally easier to do with a wider yo-yo as opposed to a narrower yo-yo. As such, the Regeneration move is easier to pull off for the people who have wider yo-yo toys. However, this is still a trick that you should be able to pull off with any yo-yo with the right amount of skill and experience.

38. Jade Whip

With this yo-yo trick, you toss the yo-yo, loop it back, then loop it again until you have the yo-yo string double-wrapped around itself and it looks like the yo-yo is in something of a sling. You then use the finger of your other free hand in order to cause the string to rotate around the yo-yo itself, which will also cause the yo-yo itself to move. You then complete the trick by making your hands move in the opposite direction and causing the yo-yo itself to spin backwards and away.

39. Magic Drop

This is a yo-yo trick that will involve you tossing the yo-yo out and then catching the string with your index finger on your free hand. You then swing the yo-yo into a cat's in the cradle position. You work the yo-yo string so that the yo-yo falls into something of a triangular position as part of a very fluid motion. If you can do all of this in what appears to be a single move, it can look very impressive in almost all cases. You just need to make the yo-yo look as bouncy as possible in order to make it work.

40. Shock Wave

With this yo-yo trick, you basically just need to figure out a way to do the Magic Drop while finding a way to add something onto it. This is one of the many yo-yo tricks that is at least partly a modification of some previous yo-yo tricks. If you can do the Magic Drop, you can do the Shock Wave yo-yo trick. You just bounce the yo-yo off into the other direction in order to complete the Magic Drop, and this is enough to make it look different in an important way. It makes the yo-yo trick slightly longer and it creates a more dramatic impression.

41. Split the Atom

This is a yo-yo trick that will seem a lot more difficult than it is. You start by throwing the yo-yo and creating a loop using your free hand. Using both hands, you more or less make the yo-yo spin back and forth in this loop so that it looks like it is on a swing set. You then try to make the loop bigger so that it looks like the yo-yo is swinging around and around in the manner of a Ferris wheel. You then sort of decrease the loop and cause the yo-yo to swing back into itself and then you retract it all and bring the yo-yo back. This is a trick that has a lot of steps, but it can work well if it exists as part of a single fluid motion.

42. Seasick

This is a trick that requires a lot of dexterity. Technically, it is not quite as hard as it looks. However, it still involves more coordination than many of the others. You start by getting the yo-yo into a configuration where it looks like it's trapped and mounted inside a long triangle. Then, you bounce the yo-yo back and forth in two different directions over the finger that is holding the triangle in place.

What makes the trick look much more impressive is when you perform this motion above your head, in front of you, and below you, and you flow between all of these three different positions all the while in one huge motion.

This requires a lot of coordination, since you have to bounce the yo-yo back over your yo-yo hand even as you are lifting the whole thing up and down in another wave motion. Basically, there's a little wave with the yo-yo itself and a big wave with your arms. If you learn how to pull off all of this smoothly and fluidly, it can be an exciting trick. You're just going to have to do it fast enough to make it work.

43. The Hook

This is a yo-yo trick that has a deceptively simple name, and it is more complicated than it might seem at first glance. You release the yo-yo in the usual way and then you loop the yo-yo string around the index finger of your free hand. From there, you swing it back and then you cross the wrists of your hands in a fluid motion.

You then cause the yo-yo to wind up in the normal manner, and this can be enough to create a somewhat confusing motion if you do it all at a fast enough rate. If you try to perform this yo-yo trick with enough grace, you will be able to make it look very impressive to most people.

44. Cold Fusion

People might find the name of this yo-yo trick intimidating, but it is a more straightforward trick than they might imagine. It is still the sort of yo-yo trick that should be considered advanced, however. You flip the yo-yo to the side in the usual way and then you catch the yo-yo string in your index finger on your non-yo-yo hand. You then work the yo-yo string into a triangular shape and you move the triangular shape from side to side and up and down and swing the yo-yo in and out of the triangular shape. You then switch the position of your hands in order to unravel the trick.

45. Kick the Bucket

This is a trick that requires a prop, and people will need strong control of their yo-yo toys in order to make it work. It involves positioning a bucket so it is within the reach of a yo-yo. From there, you swiftly throw the yo-yo in the direction of the bucket so it starts to knock the bucket over onto its side.

However, you then come at the bucket from the other side with the yo-yo after letting it roll back and then throwing it again. If you use the right amount of force, this should stop the bucket from falling over all the way, allowing you to keep the bucket in the same position. If you get skilled enough at a trick like this, you can use a lot of different props in the future.

46. Double or Nothing

With this yo-yo trick, you first throw the yo-yo and then you catch the string at the halfway point so the yo-yo is bouncing in an upward direction. You then let the yo-yo bounce down in order to create a loop using your free hand. After that, you have the yo-yo bounce upwards into the loop so that it looks as if it just landed in a small bed.

You then move your hand in the opposite direction in order to have the yo-yo bounce out of the 'bed' and up into your hands. This will cause the entire trick to unravel and it will make the yo-yo trick finish in its usual fluid motion for you. Completing this basic motion in a fluid enough manner can be impressive to see, even if it seems like it involves a lot of steps.

47. Down the Stairs

This is a fun yo-yo trick that you can practice when you're in the vicinity of a staircase. You walk down the stairs, and as you move down the stairs, you throw the yo-yo as close to the stairs as possible without actually touching them. Then, you roll the yo-yo back up again and start doing the same thing as you go down the stairs.

This will make it look as if the yo-yo is traveling up and down the stairs with you all the time as your legs are moving forward. It also demonstrates the sheer amount of control that you will have over the yo-yo as you gain more experience.

48. Boingy-Boing

With this yo-yo trick, you basically try to quickly toss the yo-yo into a nice and strong loop that you can use. You bring the actual physical yo-yo into the center of the loop and then you have the yo-yo bounce back and forth vigorously within that loop in order to make it look as if it is a bouncy ball, hence the name. Then, you jerk your hands in the opposite direction in order to undo the loop and to bring the yo-yo back to yourself. If this is something that you can pull off in a single motion, then it can work very well for you and for the people who are watching.

49. Catch the Yo-Yo

This is a fun yo-yo trick that requires a lot of coordination. You throw the yo-yo in the usual sense and then you toss the whole thing, releasing the string as well. You try to catch the yo-yo in your other hand by the string and you try to get it into Sleeper mode again, and then you repeat the process by going in something of a circle by alternating from one hand to the next. This can be a very tough trick to get right. Catching the handle of a yo-yo string is a lot harder than you might think. However, it is a trick that can work very well when it comes to entertaining the crowd in a lot of cases.

50. Kwyjibo

Fans of the classic Simpsons episodes will recognize the word Kwyjibo, which at this point in time is an actual word, contrary to what the early episode of the Simpsons said. You start by throwing the yo-yo in the usual way, and then catching the string with your free hand in a way that allows the yo-yo part to be close to your finger.

Then, you flip your hands in the other direction, so it looks like the yo-yo is caught in something of a 'cats in the cradle' position. Then, you uncross your hands, and you will then cross them in the opposite direction. Then, you roll everything back again in order to more or less undo the entire yo-yo trick.

While this appears that this is going to cause something of an uneven series of gestures, when you put all of them together, you really will end up with a yo-yo trick that is very smooth as long as you handle all of it in a really fluid manner. This is a yo-yo trick that takes a lot of control, but it can be hugely rewarding.

51. Man on the Flying Trapeze

This is a yo-yo trick that has a decent number of steps. As such, it is more about mastering the steps than dexterity here, although dexterity is still a factor. You start by throwing the yo-yo off to the side of you. Then, using your free hand, you catch the yo-yo string about halfway down the string. This will cause the yo-yo to flip towards you again.

The yo-yo will then curl over around your free hand's finger. Using this finger, you pull a loop into the yo-yo string that you are handling. You pull the loop until the loop is as long as the remainder of the yo-yo string that you have. You then let the yo-yo fall into the center of your two hands. When you bring your hands together, the yo-yo and string will have formed a combination that will strongly resemble a yo-yo on a string. It's easy to imagine that as a Man on the Flying Trapeze.

You swing the 'flying trapeze' back and forth for a few seconds, and then you withdraw your free hand quickly in the opposite direction, which should cause the yo-yo trick setup to unravel. When you can set this up and undo it in the properly fluid manner, you should be able to get the effect that you want.

52. Barrel Rolls

With this yo-yo trick, you also have to be skilled at forming quick yo-yo string triangles right away, which is just the sort of thing that can pose challenges to a lot of new yo-yo users. You release the yo-yo and then you work the string into a triangle that you will position right in front of you. You will then work the string and the yo-yo so it seems that the yo-yo is constantly changing position and moving up and down the yo-yo string in a rapid succession. This will make it appear that you are weaving the string and the yo-yo.

53. Flying Saucer

This can be a fun yo-yo trick that will be sure to entertain a lot of people. You start by making sure that the yo-yo gets into a Sleeper position parallel to the floor. The goal here is to make the string start to spin in a way that will remind you of an electric circuit going haywire or some sort of pulse. While the yo-yo is in the sleeper mode, you use your yo-yo hand to create something of a vibrating motion with the yo-yo string. This will indeed create a cool and interesting effect that will have something of a science fiction feel.

With this trick, it is truly a matter of dexterity as opposed to mastering the steps, since there are not a lot of steps here. You just have to learn the coordination that you need to make the string vibrate without knocking the yo-yo out of Sleeper mode.

54. Sleeping Beauty

With this yo-yo trick, people will probably be immediately reminded of the Flying Saucer. It is indeed similar. However, the actual vibrating string with this trick is going to be much shorter, which does create a very different effect ultimately.

This yo-yo trick involves tossing the yo-yo off to the side so that the yo-yo ends up in a Sleeper mode parallel to the ground once again. You then grab the string with your free hand so your hand is only a few inches away from the actual yo-yo. You then cause that part of the yo-yo string to vibrate, so it only looks like a small section of the string is vibrating. This might make people think of a sleeping person going through something of a trance, hence the title.

You might find that this trick is actually easier than the Flying Saucer. Making the string vibrate in the right way is easier when that is the only job of that one hand. With the Flying Saucer, you have to use the same hand to make a string vibrate and to keep the actual yo-yo in the Sleeper mode. This is a good yo-yo trick to use for practice in that way.

55. UFO

This trick is very similar to the Flying Saucer trick. However, with this trick, people should throw the yo-yo to the left of their bodies as opposed to the right, and they should try to make the vibrating string quiver at an angle.

This makes the overall yo-yo trick look a lot more mysterious in a way that should create a powerful first impression. Making the vibration waves longer will make the trick even more effective visually in most cases. Yo-yo toys already look a lot like the UFO's that people tend to see in pop culture anyway. Throwing the yo-yo at an angle helps to heighten this basic effect in many cases. It also reads as much more skillful to many of the people who are watching.

56. Sidewinder

This is another yo-yo trick that strongly resembles the UFO or the Flying Saucer. However, in this case, when people throw the yo-yo, they should then try to raise it at an angle while the string vibrates. With this yo-yo trick, you want to more or less wind up the yo-yo gradually throughout the whole trick.

However, you cause the string to vibrate so the yo-yo winds itself up in a dramatic way that appears to wobble. This is a yo-yo trick that creates a very slick effect, since it makes it look as if the person is winding up the yo-yo in a way that is very confident and assured. It also counts as a trick in its own right.

The nature of the yo-yo trick also makes it look very casual, which is part of the effect that you want to create if you are a person who is doing yo-yo tricks. You need to know what you're doing as a yo-yo trick performer, and this is a yo-yo trick that really makes you look skilled in this way.

57. Hop the Fence

With this yo-yo trick, people need to make sure that they are moving as quickly as possible. This is not a yo-yo trick that will look all that impressive if people do it slowly. However, this should not be an issue if people practice at their flips often enough.

The Hop the Fence trick is more or less a series of flips that you undertake in rapid succession of one another. Performing all of these different yo-yo tricks right in a row is enough to more or less create the impression that the yo-yo is bouncing up and down. A lot of people would say that this looks a little bit like a bunny that is hopping the fence, which can create the impression that a lot of people want with this trick.

This is one of the many yo-yo tricks where people who are right-handed or left-handed will tend to face very different issues. Left-handed people will find that the yo-yo string will keep on getting looser and looser for them if they continue to cause the yo-yo to 'hope the fence.' For people who are generally right-handed and who use their right hands as their yo-yo hands, the string is going to keep on getting tighter.

Causing the yo-yo to bounce around five times or so is usually a good start when it comes to the Hop the Fence yo-yo trick. This will create the happy medium that you need, so that you will not end up in a situation where the string will keep on getting too tight or too loose. This will create the right number of bounces.

58. Untying the Yo-Yo

This is one of the yo-yo tricks that can be complicated for the people who do not have the right level of coordination. You take two yo-yo toys and you literally loop them together, looping them both as the yo-yo strings combine with one another. You try to do this without getting the yo-yo strings tangled at all. The two different yo-yo toys should form something of a pointy shape that is reminiscent of a jack from the game of jacks.

59. Whipping the Air

You can create some interesting effects with this yo-yo trick. The important thing is to strongly bring the yo-yo back each time in order to create a lot of little bursts with it. This is part of the way that you make this trick distinctive from some of the others. While this is a trick that requires a lot of control, it is still a useful trick that can help you show off your yo-yo skills.

The Hardest Yo-Yo Tricks

These are the sorts of yo-yo tricks that are often performed by professional yo-yo players. Few people are professional yo-yo players, so you can imagine just how difficult these tricks really are. Getting hit with a yo-yo hurts more than you think. You need to be careful to make sure that you have enough control to even attempt a lot of these different yo-yo tricks. In trying to do some of them, you might actually invent your own, of course.

Some of the hardest yo-yo tricks will involve two yo-yo toys at once. You will take a risk in the process, since it will be even easier for you to hit yourself in the face as a result of these yo-yo tricks. It's much harder to control two yo-yo toys compared to one, and it doesn't even work out to say that it's twice as hard.

It's more like three times as hard, since you have to worry about the interaction between the yo-yo toys as well as the yo-yo toys themselves. You should always try to enjoy yo-yo tricks like these with caution. However, even trying these yo-yo tricks can be exhilarating, making it all the more impressive when people do actually pull them off.

60. The Yo-Yo Top

Most yo-yo tricks will involve using the yo-yo string in some way. This is a yo-yo trick that involves using the yo-yo itself in a creative way. You throw the yo-yo so it lands on the tip of your free hand's index finger. You then spin the yo-yo on the tip of that finger in the manner of a top. Then, you either wind the yo-yo back to you in the normal way, or you actually throw the string around the yo-yo and then catch the string before it falls in order to bring the yo-yo back to you.

This is actually a yo-yo trick that requires a fairly special yo-yo. You need one that is very wide and that has something of an old-fashioned or classic shape. The center needs to be thick enough that you can easily fling a string around it, basically, aiming it correctly all the while. A yo-yo that has something of an hourglass shape from the side is probably going to be the better one to use in this circumstances.

You will risk hitting your finger with a trick like this. It's also very easy to drop the yo-yo entirely, which always makes a trick look completely disappointing. This is a yo-yo trick that requires a very high degree of control at all points in time, so you can avoid missing your finger entirely and so you can prevent any other issues regarding the yo-yo trick. Still, if you can pull off a trick like this, you will succeed at impressing basically everyone who watches.

61. Arm Catch

This yo-yo trick involves creating a loop with the yo-yo string in your hands and between your two hands and then flinging the yo-yo itself to the side so it will loop on one of your arms. If you do this with enough force, the yo-yo itself will loop around your arms and land on the string loop that you have created. In order to undo the trick, you shake your arm and swiftly move it upwards. This will cause the yo-yo to bounce back.

Only some of the best yo-yo players will be able to master a trick like this one. Creating the loop in the first place can be hard enough. Getting all of these different steps to flow is very tricky. This is a yo-yo trick that requires both dexterity and the mastery of the steps, and that is a difficult combination to master. You also definitely risk getting the yo-yo string tangled up in your arm or around it. However, for the people who can pull it off, this is a great trick.

62. Double Yo-Yo Sleeper

With this yo-yo trick, you actually have to wield two different yo-yo toys at once. This trick involves more or less fleeing two yo-yo toys at once another, putting them both in the Sleeper mode. You have to toss them at one another so they don't actually knock into each other or push each other out of the Sleeper mode. This will mean knocking them under one another, over one another, and around one another.

If you do it in a steady enough flow, this will tend to create an effect that looks spectacular in its dexterity. Since you will be pulling this off in front of yourself, you will certainly be taking the risk of hitting yourself at any point during this process.

You also have to have a lot of control to do this in a way that will not just cause the yo-yo strings to get horribly tangled. This is not a yo-yo trick that a beginner or even experienced yo-yo user can try in most cases. However, as you get to be a really advanced yo-yo trick artist, you might be able to try out something that is as ambitious as this one.

63. Over the Arms

This is a trick that involves swinging the yo-yo by gripping the string fairly close to the actual yo-yo. Then, you toss the string and the yo-yo so it wraps around your arm. You then grip the yo-yo by its string and swing it. You then go behind and unravel the yo-yo from your arm in order to get it back into place.

From there, you swing it and more or less toss it onto your other arm in order to repeat the process. If you do this fluidly enough, it can look very impressive. You run the risk of tangling the yo-yo string terribly, but it can be an exciting trick to pull off.

64. Cat's Out of the Cradle

With this yo-yo trick, you get the yo-yo string into something of a cat's in the cradle type shape. You then twist the yo-yo itself in and out of the basket while moving your arms back and forth repeatedly. As your arms move back and forth, this should give you the ability to create a very fluid motion for yourself. You then gradually unravel the entire shape by reversing the direction of your movements. This is a very tough set of moves to get right, but it's something that a lot of people will love.

65. Inhale Exhale

This is a yo-yo trick that involves creating something of a basket shape for the yo-yo string and having the yo-yo itself bounce in and out of the basket shape as you move it all up and down repeatedly and cause the entire shape to shift in size and configuration. This is a yo-yo trick that should allow you to play around creatively, since it is less standardized than a good portion of the other ones that people will use today. However, it's still easy for the yo-yo string to get tangled under these circumstances.

66. Ferris Wheel

With this yo-yo trick, people take two different yo-yo toys that hopefully appear to be similar enough that they look like they could be part of the same ride. You then wrap the yo-yo strings around your free hand, but in such a way that most of the yo-yo strings are still free and they can still spin around just as easily.

Then you use the partially tied hand to cause the two different yo-yo toys to rotate in a manner that resembles a Ferris wheel. This means that they will need to be able to spin without hitting one another, which can definitely be difficult. Still, it's a great effect to try to accomplish.

67. Juggle a Yo-Yo

This is a very difficult yo-yo trick that involves crossing your arms and raising them both above your head. You will be wielding two different yo-yo toys in each hand all the while. You then bounce both yo-yo toys up and down in the normal manner.

However, since you are doing this up in the air, the yo-yo toys will appear to be going in an entirely different direction. You also need to be able to do this without having the yo-yo toys hit each other. This will make it look like you are juggling them. This is a yo-yo trick that requires you to lift these yo-yo toys against gravity, which is no easy task. With this yo-yo trick, you will need more strength than you usually would. Still, it is definitely a trick that looks very cool.

68. Rowing Yo-Yo

Here, you have another yo-yo trick that involves using two different yo-yo toys at once. As is often the case, the yo-yo toys will look better in this trick if they both look alike. You take each yo-yo in each hand and then you start to rotate them both around in circles in a manner that is similar to the Ferris Wheel trick.

However, you hold these yo-yo toys parallel to one another. To make the trick work, you time the rotation of the yo-yo toys in a way where it looks like one is more or less pushing the other into motion. Basically, one yo-yo needs to launch earlier than the other. It's very difficult to pull this one off, and it requires great dexterity and timing. You also have to be careful that you don't hit yourself. If you get the timing right, this trick is a lot of fun.

69. Yo-Yo Knot

With this yo-yo trick, you fold the string in a way that makes it resemble a cat's in the cradle knot. You then shift the knot back and forth and try to make it fluctuate so the yo-yo itself is being thrown in and out of the knot again and again. Getting the yo-yo string all tangled up in this way will be easy, but it's also worthwhile to try something like this.

70. Yo-Yo Slide

This is a yo-yo trick that involves catching the yo-yo string with your hands as you swing the yo-yo back and forth. You repeatedly fold and unravel the yo-yo string as you go, creating a very fluid motion that will make it look as if the yo-yo is repeatedly sliding around. You can repeatedly raise and lower your hands in the process. This is a trick that allows you to be flexible and improvise, which will actually make it harder than some of the tricks that are a bit more planned.

71. Caught in a Yo-Yo String

With this yo-yo trick, you will swing the yo-yo around your center as you fold the yo-yo string around your arm and then unfold the string from the other side. If you can do this in a single fluid motion or at least a series of connected motions, it will be that much easier for you to get the results that you want from this move.

It's certainly easy for the string to get caught here, and it tends to look as if you are caught in a yo-yo string anyway, hence the name. When it goes well, you're a person who appears to be good at getting caught and escaping at the same time, like a person who is skilled at handling a boa constrictor.

72. Back Loop

With a lot of the most difficult yo-yo tricks, they would technically be easy if they did not involve a particular set of obstacles. This is one of them. You do a fairly basic looping exercise with the yo-yo toys in question. However, you do this in back of you, so the yo-yo toys are adjacent to your back specifically and not to the frontal section of your body at all. This means that it is much harder to actually control the yo-yo toy when it is in action, and you might accidentally hit yourself. However, this is still a very cool trick to get right.

73. Yo-Yo Twist

This is a yo-yo trick that once again involves two yo-yo toys used at once. You hold your arms out and you spin both of the yo-yo toys next to each other. You do this so the two of them will occasionally meet by their own strings, bouncing off of one another in the process. You will spin the two of them on each side of yourself in order to complete this effect. Here, the challenge is to avoid tangling up the yo-yo strings.

74. The Looping Wheel

With this yo-yo trick, you take two yo-yo toys and start looping them against one another. One of the things that will make this yo-yo trick unique is that you start by creating a loop and then you bend and raise your body so it looks like the loop is constantly moving with you. You continue looping the two yo-yo toys as you bend and lower yourself in order to create one of the most engaging effects. If you make the yo-yo toys into looping wheels to enough of a degree, it will start to look like you are actually using something else to create a wheel, which is even more interesting to watch.

75. The Leg Loop

While this is technically a fairly simple yo-yo trick, it will be much harder than it appears to be in practice because it is one of the many very advanced yo-yo tricks that involves your body more heavily. You loop the yo-yo around in a circle in a fairly normal way. However, from there, you use your leg as an obstacle during part of the process of looping. You have to figure out how to do this in a way that is not going to injure your leg, and a leg injury is a very real risk of something like this. However, when it is done appropriately and effectively, it is a fun yo-yo trick.

76. Around the Head

This is perhaps one of the most potentially dangerous of all looping yo-yo tricks, since this one requires you to loop the yo-yo around your head. People with enough experience when it comes to looping will be able to pull something like this off, but they will risk hitting themselves in the head each time. You absolutely should not try this one without a lot of experience. However, it is still very impressive to see people looping in this way in the first place, and that can be inspiring to the people who are trying to learn how to do some of the toughest of all yo-yo tricks.

77. Loop to the Sky

With this yo-yo trick, you once again force yourself to loop it all, and it works best with two yo-yo toys that are looping in unison. However, this is a yo-yo trick where you are constantly looping upward with all of it and not just outward. You gradually rotate upwards and bring the entire looping yo-yo toys with you. As you do this, you should be reaching for the sky with these yo-yo toys at the same time. This requires a lot of power and control, but it is rewarding to achieve.

78. Equator

This is a yo-yo trick that involves maintaining two simultaneous yo-yo loops. However, you arrange the yo-yo toys in such a way that it looks like one of them is moving in a direction that makes it almost form a sphere and the other almost looks like it could create the rings of the sphere. If you move one of them fast enough, the spherical shape will be that much easier for you to form. The ring shape will be a little bit easier, but this requires you to hold your hands at very different angles in order to make it all work.

79. Looping On One Foot

This yo-yo trick is indeed exactly what it sounds like. You need to balance on one foot while performing the yo-yo trick and you need to loop the yo-yo around the leg that is balancing off of the ground. This is definitely a tough sort of trick, and you need to be able to stand on your foot for a long period of time in order to make it work. Looping around your foot is tough, and you need to avoid hitting yourself. Still, it is a cool yo-yo trick to see.

80. Colorful Flow

You will actually need to get specialized yo-yo toys in order to make this one really work. This is a trick that features yo-yo toys more or less playing off of one another so it looks like they are part of a continuous organism. If the yo-yo toys feature glow-in-the-dark effects and it's dark, that will make this trick look even more impressive. You need to maintain a steady flow in order to make it work, but this can make all they difference.

81. Dribbling Yo-Yo

This is a yo-yo trick that involves looping the yo-yo toys in the direction of the ground in a fairly continuous motion. You will look almost like you are dribbling a basketball in that way. If you have the yo-yo toys pointed in the right direction and if you are causing the yo-yo toys to bounce in the right way, this can give the yo-yo trick a great deal of energy right away. You can make it look like the toys are moving on their own in a way.

82. Catch the Yo-Yo

You will once again use two yo-yo toys for the sake of this yo-yo trick. You will loop them, but this time, as you are looping them, you need to catch each yo-yo as it comes to you. If you do this in a fluid enough pattern, it is enough to create the impression that these are spheres and not yo-yo toys at all, but the yo-yo effect will still be there. You can show off your hand-eye coordination with a move like this one, and it does carry with it the risk that you might accidentally hit yourself.

83. Inventing the Wheel

This is a yo-yo trick that is similar to some of the yo-yo tricks that involve the creation of wheels. However, in this case, the strings of the two different yo-yo toys will actually mingle together and you will be able to use them in order to create something that looks like the spokes of a wheel in the process. If you move the wheel in front of you fast enough and it really is revolving, it will actually look a little bit like a real wheel. Yo-yo strings can look enough like the spokes of a wheel that the trick can really work.

84. Concentric Circles

This is another yo-yo trick that involves the quick creation of a wheel. However, in this case, the goal is to make the wheel get smaller and smaller and then larger and larger through the creative handling of the yo-yo strings. This is a yo-yo trick that requires the firm knowledge of whether or not the strings can be tightened using a certain method or not, but it is very much the sort of thing that people can learn with time.

85. Yo-Yo Cyclone

This is a yo-yo trick that starts out with the two yo-yo toys playing off one another in a loop. However, what you do is you pull the strings closer and closer together until the point where the yo-yo toys are looping on top of one another and they look like they are part of the same object, in a way. If you do this with yo-yo toys that will glow in the dark in any way, that will make the whole experience all that much better. Pulling the strings tightly in a way where it does not cause the yo-yo toys to stop spinning is an issue, but it can be done.

86. Roller Coaster

You can loop with this yo-yo trick, and this yo-yo trick requires looping very broadly while spinning around. This will make a lot of people think of a roller coaster, hence the name. The hard part here is basically moving your body at the right time so you do not hit yourself at any point. This can be a fun trick, but it is a trick that requires you to be coordinated all throughout your body and not in the most obvious ways. It is a trick that is worth it if you can get it right.

87. Reach for the Sky

This is a yo-yo trick that actually involves a fairly simple motion. You more or less bounce and retract the yo-yo in the normal way upwards. However, you do this at a more challenging angle than you usually would and you keep trying to raise the yo-yo higher each time while another lower yo-yo appears to be challenging that one to new heights at a different level. Finding a way to strike the balance between the two of them can be difficult, but it is worth pursuing.

88. Untying the Yo-Yo

With this yo-yo trick, you are using your neck as a prop. This is definitely not a trick that people will want to try lightly. You more or less cause the yo-yo to loop and creatively handle the yo-yo as it is on your neck, looping the yo-yo in and out of itself before completely releasing it. This is a yo-yo trick that can be very difficult to pull off in some cases, and it is a risky trick to perform. You need to keep a pair of scissors handy in order to make sure that you have some sort of recourse before something happens with a potential yo-yo accident.

89. Looping Through the Arm

You cause the yo-yo to loop in this trick, but you use your entire free arm as a prop. This means that the yo-yo is repeatedly looping through your arm in order to increase the level of challenge that you will experience as a result. You will need to be good at creating a yo-yo loop with a single hand, and this is not something that all people can do even if they have a lot of experience with a given yo-yo trick. Still, this is something that can be fun to master, although you might want to have some safety scissors handy all the while.

90. Yo-Yo the String

This is a fun yo-yo trick where the string and the yo-yo more or less switch places. You start out by throwing the yo-yo in the normal way and then you catch the yo-yo by the yo-yo itself as opposed to the string. Then, you use the string and only the string in order to create a lot of the different looping effects that you want. This is the sort of thing that can be difficult to perform in a lot of cases, and even making the catches that you need can be tricky in most cases. Still, it is fun to see something of a role reversal with regards to the use of a yo-yo and everything else.

91. Wrap Around

With this yo-yo trick, you try to get the yo-yo wrapped around a somewhat distant obstacle before switching your arm motion in order to unravel it and causing it to retreat. Finding a way to do this with most yo-yo toys will be tough, since there is a strong possibility that you are going to end up getting the yo-yo all tangled. Still, it is possible, and there are plenty of great yo-yo tricks that involve props in this category.

92. No Strings Attached

You will need a special yo-yo in order to make this yo-yo trick work, of course. This is a trick involving releasing the yo-yo from its string as you throw it, and then catching it again by the center of it using the string. Essentially, you are linking the yo-yo back to its string in midair. This is the sort of thing that is very difficult to perform. It might be even more difficult than it looks. If you don't have the special yo-yo that a string free operation will require, then the trick is not going to work at all. However, while this is a technically simple trick, it reads as awesome to everyone who sees it and it is a huge crowd pleaser.

93. Yo-Yo Ball

This is another yo-yo trick that will require a special yo-yo that is capable of performing a lot of different stringless tricks. You throw the yo-yo and release it from its string and then you quickly wrap the string around your neck so the string still has a lot of 'arms' that you can use on either side. You then bounce the yo-yo quickly off of both strings before you try to bounce that yo-yo back onto its original string after you take the string off of your neck. It's hard to overstate the difficulty of a yo-yo trick like this one. However, it is still a yo-yo trick that a lot of people will absolutely love to see when it is done well.

94. One With the Yo-Yo

This is a trick that will work well with a stringless special yo-yo as well as a more standard yo-yo. You loop the yo-yo around your neck and then you spin around while trying to keep the yo-yo above your head, making sure that the yo-yo is not going to be able to hit your head in the process. It is possible that people will have the yo-yo bounce off of their heads over the course of practicing a trick like this one. It is a good idea to get a really light yo-yo for a yo-yo trick like this. Still, it is very cool when people do it, partly because of the nature of the risk involved.

95. Spinning Plate Yo-Yo

You need props for this yo-yo trick as well, and this becomes increasingly common for a good portion of the very difficult yo-yo tricks. You need to throw the yo-yo so the actual yo-yo lands on a wand at the top of the wand. Then, try to keep the yo-yo spinning in a consistent direction so it is balancing on the top of the wand the entire time. The kinetic energy for the yo-yo still needs to come from you, which is part of the challenge. Making the yo-yo land in the right way is also a hard part. However, this is a versatile yo-yo trick that looks very interesting visually.

96. A Trio

While this is technically a yo-yo trick that involves a simple move, there is no such thing as a simple yo-yo trick that involves three yo-yo toys. You try to wield three different yo-yo toys at once in this trick, allowing yourself to find a way to get them to get in sync with one another. It can work better if you use your dominant hand as the yo-yo hand that holds two yo-yo toys instead of one. If you can keep this many yo-yo toys steady at once, it will be that much more impressive.

97. Newton's Cradle

People are used to seeing the Newton's cradle toy on office desks. This is a fun toy that demonstrates the conservation of energy as you watch these balls knock into one another and then knock back, seemingly moving on their own. With this trick, you try to create a similar effect with looping yo-yo toys. Adding three different yo-yo toys can help to make this trick look that much more impressive in all cases. Getting them into the initial setup will often be the harder part, since the actual yo-yo toys will eventually be able to sustain their own momentum.

98. Knee Bounce

This is another yo-yo trick that involves two yo-yo toys. In this case, you try to work it so the yo-yo toys are bouncing off of your knees into one another and that they are able to use that momentum to sustain this pattern. This will almost look as if the two yo-yo toys are jumping off of your knee, and this is a fun effect to create in a lot of cases. You just have to find a way to get them going.

99. Grid Iron

With this yo-yo trick, you do a series of loops that create a pattern where the yo-yo string looks like it has formed a ladder. This requires a lot of subtle loops, throws, and bounces in order to make it all work. The shape that the yo-yo string will form will tend to be interesting in most cases. This is certainly more of a string trick as opposed to a trick that involves the yo-yo itself. Still, it is a tough and impressive string trick that a lot of people will want to see.

100. Scooter Trick

This is a yo-yo trick that involves causing the yo-yo to bounce in and out of a series of different string shapes. You cause it to develop a cat's cradle and then another one that is perpendicular to the first one. This can cause the yo-yo string to develop something of a scooter shape. The process might remind people of the set of steps that people will use in order to create balloon animals. Watching the yo-yo get into the right position in the first place is really entertaining in most cases.

Conclusion

Some of these yo yo tricks should be relatively easy to learn. Others will be so difficult that only the professionals will really be able to do them. There are professional yo-yo players in the modern world, and they will have the practice that it takes to pull off some of the hardest of all tricks. However, people who enjoy yo-yo tricks as a hobby can take on the challenge of learning every single one of these tricks if that is what they want. They might have to be careful with some of them. However, all of them can be entertaining to see as well as entertaining to learn.

Milton Keynes UK
Ingram Content Group UK Ltd.
UKHW021257041123
431960UK00021B/596